Animal Mash-Ups

D0927160

VICKY FRANCHINO

Children's Press®
An Imprint of Scholastic Inc.

Content Consultant
Dr. Stephen S. Ditchkoff
Professor of Wildlife Sciences
Auburn University
Auburn, Alabama

Library of Congress Cataloging-in-Publication Data

Franchino, Vicky, author.
 Animal mash-ups / by Vicky Franchino.
   pages cm. — (True books)
 Summary: "Learn all about nature's most incredible hybrids, from those that occur naturally to those created with the help of scientists and breeders" — Provided by publisher.
 Includes bibliographical references and index.
 ISBN 978-0-531-21544-9 (library binding) — ISBN 978-0-531-21581-4 (pbk.)
 1. Animal breeding—Juvenile literature. 2. Rare breeds—Juvenile literature. I. Title. II. Series: True book.
 SF105.F73 2016
 636.08'2—dc23   2015015433

Front cover: A zonkey, a cross between a zebra and a donkey

Back cover: A liger, a cross between a lion and a tiger

Find the Truth!

Everything you are about to read is true *except* for one of the sentences on this page.

Which one is **TRUE**?

T or F   Animal hybrids can only be created with help from humans.

T or F   Some animal hybrids can have babies.

Find the answers in this book.

Contents

THE BIG TRUTH!

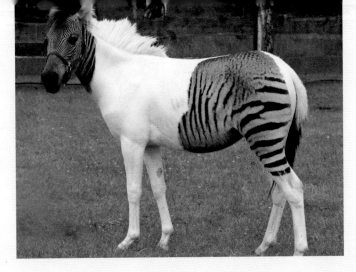

A zorse is a hybrid of a zebra and a horse.

4 Are Hybrids Good or Bad?

How might a hybrid be like
an invasive species? **39**

Puggles need lots of exercise. Plan to take lots of long walks with this dog!

CHAPTER 1

Real or Make-Believe?

Have you ever wondered what it would be like to combine the cool features of different animals to make a brand-new creature? Fairy tales, myths, and science-fiction stories are filled with examples of animal "mash-ups," or **hybrids**. But can these creatures really exist? You might be surprised to learn that the answer is sometimes yes—though maybe not exactly the way you imagined!

Some representations of a sphinx include elements of a human, lion, bird, and serpent.

What Is a Hybrid?

A hybrid is a combination of two different things. You might have heard this word used to describe a vehicle. Hybrid cars run on both electricity and gasoline. Living creatures can be hybrids, too. They are created when organisms with different **DNA** come together and create a new animal or plant. DNA is a material in the cells of every plant and animal. It is a code that controls an organism's features.

DNA is responsible for this person's blue eyes.

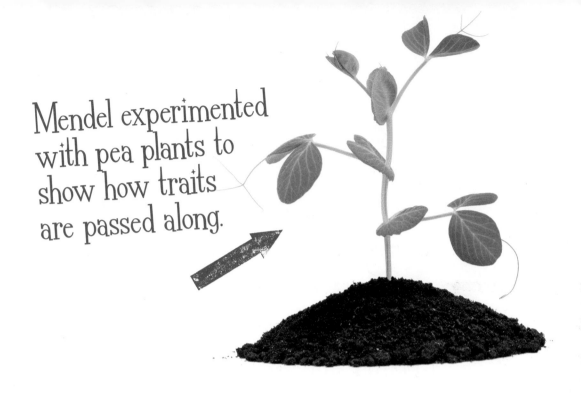

Mendel experimented with pea plants to show how traits are passed along.

Plant Hybrids

Scientist Gregor Mendel was one of the first to discover that a living organism passes **traits** on to the next generation. He found that tall plants had tall "children." He also learned that he could create different results when he mixed the cells of tall and short plants. Today, scientists use his ideas to create hybrid plants that grow faster, produce tastier fruit, and resist insects.

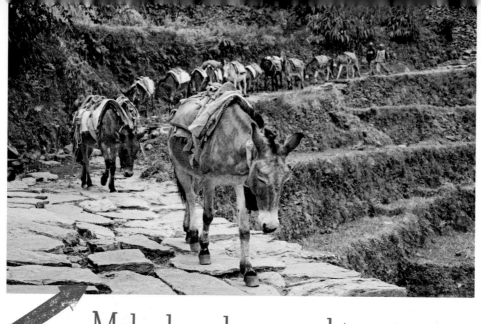

Mules have been used in mining, to build railroads, and in war.

One of the First Animal Hybrids

There are hybrid animals, too, although they are less common than hybrid plants. Most happen with a little—or a lot—of human help. Mules were one of the first hybrid animals. They have been around for thousands of years. Mules are the **offspring** of a male donkey and a female horse. These hybrids are smart, strong, and nimble. Mules can pull heavy loads and walk safely on narrow trails.

No Babies

A species is a group of plants or animals that can **breed** with one another. When two different species breed, their offspring is usually sterile. This means the offspring cannot have babies. As a result, the unique **genes** created by mixing two species are not passed to another generation. In some rare cases, hybrids can have babies. But there usually is not another hybrid to **mate** with, and the unique genes eventually disappear.

It is unlikely that these kittens, a hybrid of a white Bengal tiger and an African white lion, will ever have babies of their own.

Hybrids and Change

Animal species evolve, or change, slowly over a long period of time. Can hybridization help species evolve more quickly? Scientists are not sure. If hybrids are **isolated** from their parent species and can mate with other hybrids, this can create a new species. This new species might have characteristics that would have taken many years to develop otherwise.

Some scientists argue that the great skua may be the result of a cross between two other bird species long ago.

Mother Nature's Hybrids

Although humans create most hybrids, some happen naturally. Zonkeys, zedonks, and zorses are hybrids of either a zebra and a donkey or a zebra and a horse. When they live in the same area, zebras, donkeys, and horses have been known to mate and produce these hybrid babies.

A wholphin (left) pops its head above the water next to a bottlenose dolphin.

CHAPTER 2

The Wild World of Hybrids

In 1985, a bottlenose dolphin at a sea park in Hawaii gave birth to a baby that did not look quite like a dolphin. The caretakers at the park were very surprised. Who was the father? It was a false killer whale that shared the dolphin's enclosure. Caretakers called the baby a wholphin. The wholphin's coloring, size, and number of teeth were a mix of both parents.

 Hybrid names are usually a combination of the names of its parents' species.

Ligers have spots, stripes, and short manes.

Ligers and Tigons

A movie character once said a liger was his favorite animal. Ligers might sound like a joke, but they are real! Ligers are the offspring of a male lion and a female tiger. Tigons have a tiger father and a lion mother. These hybrids only happen when humans are involved. Lions and tigers would not come together in the wild. The first ligers may have been born more than 200 years ago.

Leopons

If lions and tigers can mate with each other, it seems reasonable to assume other big cats could, too. Whether that is true is a bit of a mystery. However, some private zoos and animal parks say other feline hybrids exist. For instance, the Koshien Hanshin Park in Japan is supposedly the birthplace of male and female leopons. These animals had a leopard father and a lion mother.

Koshien Hanshin Park's leopons rest in their enclosure.

Pizzlies and Grolar Bears

Two of the world's scariest animals are grizzly bears and polar bears. Put them together and you get one terrifying beast! With recent **climate change**, Earth's average temperature has been rising. The polar ice caps where polar bears spend much of their time have been melting. As this happens, grizzly bears have moved north. Polar bears have headed south. When these bears cross paths, they sometimes mate. The result is called a pizzly or grolar bear.

The first report of a wild pizzly bear was in 2006.

Lynxes (left) and bobcats (right) are closely related species. As a result, some blynx can have kittens.

Blynx

The grolar is not the only animal created by climate change. As warmer temperatures push the bobcat north, it sometimes mates with the Canada lynx. The result is an animal known as a blynx. This hybrid has been found in the United States in Maine and Minnesota, and in New Brunswick, Canada. Government researchers used DNA testing to prove the animal was a true hybrid.

Coywolves are larger than an average coyote.

Backyard Hybrids

Think hybrids only live in zoos or the wild? The coywolf might live in your backyard! This creature is likely part gray or red wolf and part coyote, but scientists are not entirely sure. Those animals do not usually get along. The coywolf lives in the eastern part of North America, in both rural and urban areas. It has strong jaws and travels in packs like a wolf. It is an opportunistic feeder, like a coyote, eating whatever it comes across.

Beefalo

Beef is a popular food in the United States, but cattle are expensive to raise. Scientists had a solution: the beefalo. This hybrid combines bison and bovine—also known as cattle! Bison are strong, have an easy time giving birth, and grow quickly. Cattle are easy to handle, and some types can be milked. Meat from a beefalo is naturally leaner and healthier than regular beef and less expensive for the farmer to raise.

Any kind of cattle can be mixed with bison to create beefalo.

A Hybrid Surprise

The origin of the clymene dolphin has long been a mystery. It leaps like a spinner dolphin, but its skull is shaped like a striped dolphin's. To solve the puzzle, scientists studied this dolphin's DNA and discovered something interesting: It is a hybrid! New animal species like this can occur in nature when two species mate and their offspring live in isolation and mate with other hybrids.

The clymene dolphin is the first known hybrid marine mammal.

Camas are a hybrid of llamas (left) and camels (right).

The Cama

A cama is a combination of a camel and a llama. It could never exist in nature because its parents live on different continents. The camel lives in Asia, and the llama lives in South America. Scientists who bred the cama hoped it would have a mild spirit like the llama and the power of a camel. They got the strength they wanted but were not so lucky with the mood. Camas are quite cranky!

Bonobos (left) and chimpanzees (right) might have created a hybrid in the past.

Bonanzees

You probably know what a chimpanzee is. But have you heard of a bonobo? It is a primate that's a close cousin of the chimpanzee. Scientists believe chimpanzees and bonobos probably mated at one time and created a hybrid called a bonanzee. Because bonanzees later mated with chimpanzees or bonobos, instead of other bonanzees, this hybrid disappeared. Scientists can still find DNA evidence of it when they look at today's chimps and bonobos.

What Is Happening to the Cuban Crocodiles?

Cuban crocodiles are in danger of **extinction**. Farming has made their freshwater homes salty. The crocodiles are also mating with American crocodiles instead of each other, creating a hybrid. Soon there may be no Cuban crocodiles left. Scientists studied the DNA of crocodiles they thought were Cuban. They discovered many were actually a Cuban-American hybrid. This hybrid can survive in the salty water. Could this mean the end of the Cuban crocodile?

Some hybrids, such as the Cuban-American crocodile, can survive where the parent species cannot.

Genes Are Not Everything

One day in 1921, a schoolteacher named Hans Duncker heard an enchanting sound as he walked the city streets of Bremen, Germany: the call of a nightingale. He was extremely confused, however. It was the wrong time of year for nightingales. Plus, the birds were only found in the country. Duncker tracked the source of the song and discovered a shopkeeper named Karl Reich. Reich had created a canary-nightingale hybrid.

Duncker was fascinated by the idea of making an animal with specific traits. He dreamed of creating a bright red canary. Breeders knew they could change a canary's color by breeding different types of this bird. Duncker and Reich wondered if they could create a new canary color by breeding canaries with other bird species.

Duncker and Reich picked the red siskin to breed with a canary. The two men succeeded in creating an orange canary. However, they were never able to darken the color to red. This is because they only focused on the birds' genes. Food and environment can also change an animal's coloring. Later researchers tried feeding canary-siskin hybrids carotene. This is the substance that makes carrots orange. It was a success! The carotene turned the birds bright red.

CHAPTER 3

Hundreds of Hybrids

Go into a pet store or visit a pet Web site. You will quickly see that there are many types of hybrid pets. Why do people create hybrids? Usually they are trying to make a "better" animal. Purebred animals, which are from just one breed, sometimes have health problems or are jumpy or unfriendly. Hybrid breeders claim they can create animals that are smarter, calmer, less likely to shed hair, and cute, too!

 Dogs with DNA from two or more breeds are sometimes called mutts.

Just Add a Poodle

What do labradoodles, cockapoos, and schnoodles share? They are all part poodle. The poodle is a very common choice when creating a hybrid dog. Poodles are known for being smart, athletic, and having a good personality. They also

shed less than many breeds. This makes them good for people with allergies—or who do not like dog hair all over their house!

Cockapoos are a hybrid of poodles and cocker spaniels.

The word dachshund means "badger dog" in German.

"Weiner" Dogs

Nicknamed after the sausage they resemble, dachshunds are a combination of hounds and terriers. This hybrid has been around for a long time. Some sources say the first dachshunds were bred in the 1800s and 1900s. Other sources go back as far as the 1500s. Dachshunds were originally bred to hunt badgers. Their short legs let them crawl through tunnels, and their paws are good for digging. Dachshunds are also good at tracking and hunting.

Puggles are one of the most popular hybrid pets.

Puggles

Puggles are a mix of beagles and pugs. These dogs are cute, smart, and very energetic. They also love to eat (and eat!) and need lots of exercise each day. Puggles are extremely friendly, and they like lots of company. One downside of their nature is that they may bark a lot when they are left alone, because they prefer to be with people.

Good Gollie!

Gollies are a mix of golden retrievers and collies. They are family friendly and easy to train. They are also smart, patient, and loyal. Gollies typically live more than a decade and are a fairly large breed. They can weigh up to 75 pounds (34 kilograms)! Unfortunately, gollies can have a lot of health issues. Both parent breeds can have problems with their hips, eyes, and heart, so gollies can, too.

Gollies have long, thick fur and need frequent brushing.

Chocolate Cat

The color of this cat's fur is simply delicious. Many people think it looks like chocolate! The Havana Brown cat is a mix of a black cat and a Siamese, with a little bit of Russian Blue mixed in. Although many cats have a reputation for wanting to be alone, the Havana Brown is quite social and likes to play. This cat was first bred in England in the 1950s.

Havana Browns are bred to have green eyes.

Tonkinese cats like to talk and talk. Prepare to listen!

Mink Coat

This beautiful cat looks like it is wearing a warm mink coat. The Tonkinese is a combination of Siamese and Burmese cats. Tonkinese come in many color combinations. Many of these cats have blue eyes, like their Siamese ancestors. Others have green or even aqua-colored eyes. This cat is smart and friendly. It likes to play, and it likes to cuddle, too.

This ocicat is named after the wild cat it resembles: the ocelot.

Jungle Cat

Look quickly and you might think this cat is a miniature leopard or another wild jungle cat. A mix of Siamese, Abyssinian, and American shorthair, the ocicat was first bred in the 1960s. The original breeder wanted to create a cat that looked like its wild cousins but acted like a domestic pet. This cat comes in a number of spot and color combinations.

A Wild Idea

Some animal lovers like the idea of mixing a wild cat with a domestic one. The Savannah, Chausie, and toyger (below) are all examples of this. Unfortunately, in many cases this experiment has not gone very well. These hybrids might never learn to use a litter box. They sometimes become quite wild as they get older. Many also have health problems.

CHAPTER 4

Are Hybrids Good or Bad?

It is hard to say if hybrids are good or bad. Many people worry hybrids will act like an invasive species. This is a plant or animal that does not occur naturally in an area and is brought in from the outside. Sometimes these species attack native species or use their resources. Native plants and animals sometimes disappear when an invasive species moves in.

Despite some being owned as pets, wolf-dog hybrids can be dangerous.

Who Will Survive?

In the wild, salmon sometimes mate with brown trout and produce offspring. When researchers created a hybrid of these fish in a lab, they found that the new fish grew very quickly. The hybrids competed with natural salmon for food and usually won because of their size. People are concerned that these hybrids could destroy the "real" salmon.

Salmon in the lab grew faster when crossed with the brown trout (below).

A dzo is a yak-cattle hybrid often used in the Himalayas as a pack animal.

The Best of Both

Hybrids can be a good way to combine the best features of two types of animals. For instance, donkeys crossed with zebras—called zonkeys—can work harder than regular donkeys in hot weather because zebras are used to a hot climate. Beefalos are as hardy as bison, with the delicious flavor of beef. There are many dog hybrids and cat hybrids. Some mixes are designed not to shed fur. Others might be good for owners who have allergies.

A zonkey named Telegraph was born at a zoo in Crimea in 2014.

Hybrids at the Zoo

Should zoos create hybrids? Some people believe it is okay to create a hybrid to learn about animal characteristics. Others think zoos should focus on existing animal species and how they live in the natural world. Though people thought hybrids would be healthier than other animals, they can actually have more health problems. This is another reason why some people believe it is a mistake to create them.

Animals and Humans

True animal-human hybrids are found only in science-fiction books. However, scientists have created animal-human **chimeras**, organisms with cells from two species. Human cells have been put into mice to help predict how a human's organs might react to medication. Animal cells have been used to grow replacement organs, such as heart valves and ligaments, for humans. Some scientists wonder if it is good or bad to do this kind of research. What do you think? ★

Scientists often use mice to learn about hybrids and animal-human chimeras.

Number of teeth in a wholphin's mouth: 66, compared to a dolphin's 44 and a whale's 88

Weight of a liger: As much as a lion and tiger combined, roughly 0.5 tons (453 kg)

Amount of raw meat a liger can eat in a day: Up to 30 lb. (13.6 kg)

Distance a coywolf can travel in a day: 10 to 15 mi. (16 to 24 km)

Percentage of a beefalo's DNA that comes from bison: About 38 percent

Number of types of hybrid dogs: More than 500

Weight of a dachshund: 9 to 35 lb. (4 to 15.8 kg)

Did you find the truth?

(F) Animal hybrids can only be created with help from humans.

(T) Some animal hybrids can have babies.

Resources

Book

Simpson, Kathleen. *Genetics: From DNA to Designer Dogs*. Washington, DC: National Geographic, 2008.

Important Words

breed (BREED) — to mate and give birth to young

chimeras (kye-MEER-az) — individuals, organs, or parts made up of tissues from two different species

climate change (KLYE-mit CHAYNJ) — global warming and other changes in the weather and weather patterns that are happening because of human activity

DNA (dee-en-AY) — the molecule found inside every cell in the body, containing information on how each cell should work

extinction (ik-STINGK-shuhn) — complete disappearance of a species from a certain area or from the entire world

genes (JEENZ) — one of the parts of a cell; genes passed from parents to children determine how the children look and the way they grow

hybrids (HYE-bridz) — plants or animals that have parents of two different species

isolated (EYE-suh-late-id) — kept alone or separate

mate (MAYT) — to join together to produce babies

offspring (AWF-spring) — the young of an animal

traits (TRAYTS) — qualities or characteristics that make one person or thing different from another

Index

Page numbers in **bold** indicate illustrations.

About the Author

The only hybrid animals that Vicky Franchino had heard about before writing this book were dogs, cats, and beefalo (which she has never tried). Her sister has a cockapoo named Bella that she is very fond of. Vicky is happy to report that Bella doesn't shed very much and has a very nice personality—just like this hybrid is supposed to! Vicky has written many books about animals and enjoys learning new things about them. She lives in Madison, Wisconsin, with her family and is not planning to get a hybrid pet any time soon!

Photo by Kat Franchino